A souvenir guide

Croome
Worcestershire

Matt Shinn

C000183048

National Trust

Foreword

Welcome to Croome, the home of the Coventry family for over four hundred years.

I was not born at Croome and, indeed, the possibility of my succeeding to the title was remote. During my childhood my family moved from England to East Africa, where I spent my teenage years. Our house there was named 'Croome', so I was always aware of my connection with this historic place. It was in 2004, because of the sad early death of the then heir, the last of a line, that I became 13th Earl of Coventry.

Any visit to Croome will be dominated by my ancestor, George William Coventry, 6th Earl, as it was through his own genius in recognising the potential genius in others that we have all we see today. His input was considerable and the outcome was a collaboration between himself and men such as Capability Brown, Robert Adam and James Wyatt, who, under Coventry's guidance, worked to form the 'total work of art' that Croome became.

Throughout the 19th century, Croome was preserved and nurtured by the 9th Earl; he was born in 1838 and died at the age of 92. It is through his devotion to the place that Croome today is almost exactly what his great-great-grandfather left to us.

In 1921 the 9th Earl set up the Croome Estate Trust in order to ensure that the 15,000 acre estate would be preserved. However, in 1939, fate and the tragic circumstances of the Second World War intervened. The 10th Earl, having volunteered when war was declared, was killed in the retreat to Dunkirk. A whole new chapter began when, after the war was over, such houses were no longer viable and Croome Court had to be sold.

The place became a school, a retreat for the Hare Krishna movement and the base for the ambitions of various property developers. Finally, in 2004 when it was once again on the market, the Croome Estate Trust were in a position to buy back my family's ancestral home, which had always been their ambition. They leased it to the National Trust for 999 years, so re-combining the house with its parkland.

Let me end with a heartfelt thank you to the National Trust. Without their hard work, knowledge and commitment, we would not now be able to celebrate the history of Croome and I look forward to the future with interest and excitement.

George Coventry, 13th Earl

Right The Coventry coat of arms, courtesy of Worcestershire Archive & Archaeology Service

The Coventrys of Croome

Sir Thomas Coventry (1547–1606) *acquires Croome d'Abitot 1592* = Margaret Jeffery

Thomas, 1st Baron (1578–1640) Lord Keeper = (1) Sarah Sebright m. 1606
= (2) Elizabeth Pitchford m. 1610

Walter = Susanna West

Thomas, 2nd Baron (1606–61) = Mary Craven (d. 1634) m. 1627

George, 3rd Baron = Margaret Tufton
(1628–80) | (1636–1729) m. 1653

Thomas, 5th Baron (1629–99) = (1) Winifred Edgcumbe (d. 1694)
cr. 1st Earl 1697 | = (2) Elizabeth Grimes (d. 1724) m. 1695

John, 4th Baron (1654–87)

Thomas, 2nd Earl (1663–1710) = Anne Somerset (1673–1763) m. 1691

Gilbert, 4th Earl = (1) Dorothy Keyte (d. 1707) m. 1694
(1668–1719) = (2) Anne Masters (1691–1788) m. 1715

Thomas, 3rd Earl (1702–12)

William, 5th Earl (1678–1751) = Elizabeth Allen (d. 1738) m. 1719

Thomas Henry, Viscount Deerhurst (1720–44)

George William, 6th Earl = (1) Maria Gunning (1732–60) m. 1752
(1722–1809) = (2) Barbara St John (1737–1804) m. 1764

John Bulkeley (1724–1801)

George William, 7th Earl (1758–1831) = (1) Catherine Henley (c. 1760–79) m. 1777
= (2) Peggy Pitches (d. 1840)

George William, 8th Earl = (1) Emma Lygon (d. 1810) m. 1808
(1784–1843) | = (2) Mary Beauclerk (1791–1845) m. 1811

Hon. William James Coventry (1797–1877)
(5th son of 7th Earl)

George William, Viscount Deerhurst (1808–38) = Harriet Cockerell (d. 1842) m. 1836

George William, 9th Earl (1838–1930) = Blanche Craven (1842–1930) m. 1865

William George (1826–1874)

George William, Viscount Deerhurst (1865–1927) = Virginia Bonynge (b. 1866) m. 1894

Gilbert William (1868–1947)

George William, 10th Earl = Nesta Donne Philipps m. 1921
(1900–40)

Charles = Lily Whitehouse

Cecil Dick Bluett Coventry (1905–1952)

George William, 11th Earl (1934–2002)

Francis, 12th Earl (1912–2004)

George William Bluett Coventry,
13th Earl (b. 1939)

Peter Harold Sherwood Coventry
(1941–1985)

Lady Diana Elizabeth Sherwood Coventry
(b. 1980)

David Duncan Sherwood Coventry
(b. 1973) *Heir presumptive*

A Paradise on English Soil

The balanced and orderly Palladian mansion at Croome is surrounded by one of Britain's finest 18th-century landscape gardens. It is an Arcadian scene, with gently rolling meadows, a winding river and lake, groves of trees and Neo-classical garden buildings, all set against the backdrop of the Malvern Hills.

It seems like a natural idyll, but this is in fact a man-made landscape. It was largely the vision of a single man, George William, the 6th Earl of Coventry. Croome is testimony to his passion for the latest styles in architecture and landscape design, and his great ability to spot talent in the people he chose to work with. Croome was Lancelot 'Capability' Brown's first complete landscape, and his first major architectural project. Croome also saw Robert Adam's first important commission. This was a seminal work in the careers of both future masters of 18th-century design. Croome was to be the template for what they would both go on to achieve throughout the country.

Back to nature

Croome launched the career of 'Capability' Brown, the man who is still revered as Britain's foremost garden designer. The English landscape garden, which has been called one of the country's greatest contributions to the visual arts, was his signature style. Together, the 6th Earl and his designers made something extraordinary here, and it was copied again and again, throughout Britain and beyond.

The story of Croome, however, doesn't end with the 18th century. What happened to the park and mansion subsequently makes this place even more interesting. There was a secret wartime airbase here, a school for disadvantaged boys, and a Hare Krishna college. All left their mark on the building and landscape that we see today.

From 1996, after decades of neglect, Croome has been the site of one of the National Trust's biggest repair projects. The work was carried out while the house and park were still open to the public and with more restoration work to do in the future, visitors will continue to see Croome grow and change.

Left The Temple Greenhouse sits harmoniously within the landscape

Right Croome Court viewed from the pasture

The 'noble improver': The 6th Earl

Croome was shaped by the taste and talents of a single individual.

George William, the 6th Earl of Coventry, was only 28 when he inherited Croome Court in 1751. His elder brother, Thomas Henry, had died in 1744 at the age of 23 so it had been something of a surprise to inherit. The loss of his brother left George William distraught – 'if I could be sever'd into two,' he wrote, 'and one part left alive and the other part taken away, the separation could not be greater. He was indeed the better half.'

The brothers had been very close, and had frequently discussed their ideas on architecture and garden design. So when George William became heir, he was determined to realise the vision that he had shared with his brother, and turn Croome into the epitome of contemporary style. It was to be his lifetime's work. He added the finishing touches around fifty years later, having spent some £400,000 (the equivalent of about £35 million in today's money).

Risk-taker

Where did the 6th Earl get his ideas from? Unlike many of the landowners who became patrons of landscape designers in the 18th century, he never undertook the Grand Tour of Europe. He loved Paris, however, and French furniture and porcelain in particular. Indeed, the 6th Earl was one of the first Englishmen to go to Paris after the Seven Years War. This willingness to take risks earned him a place at the forefront of fashion, a position that was particularly evident in his interior design choices at Croome.

Left Plant bills

Far left George William,
6th Earl of Coventry, by
Allan Ramsay c.1765

In George William's case though, his interest in the latest developments in design seems to have been mixed with a certain obsessiveness as a collector, and competitiveness too. He had to have the grandest, the rarest, and the most beautiful of everything. Fortunately for him, he had the wealth to satisfy his whims, and at least to equal any rival.

Nevertheless, the 6th Earl was always keen to secure the best value for his money, often querying tradesmen's bills. He was also meticulous, keeping every bill and receipt, many of which are now in the archive at the Worcestershire Archive Service at the Hive in Worcester.

Tempests and tactlessness

The 6th Earl and his first wife, the famous beauty Maria Gunning, made a glamorous couple, though relations were not always harmonious between them. During their honeymoon, the 6th Earl is said to have chased Maria round a dinner table with a napkin, trying to wipe off the rouge that she was wearing. Maria was also famous for her lack of tact. When George II asked her what she would most like to see in London, she is said to have replied 'a coronation!'

Death by make-up?

Maria Gunning wore lead-based make-up, which contributed to her death by making her vulnerable to tuberculosis. She succumbed aged only 28. It is said that she died by the light of a tea kettle with the shutters of her room in Croome Court closed, so that people couldn't see her once beautiful, but now ravaged, face.

Landscape as Art

There's much more to Croome's landscape garden than meets the eye...

The landscape at Croome was not made as an afterthought. House and garden here form an integrated design. The park may be in the naturalistic style, based partly on the landscape paintings of Claude Gellée 'le Lorrain' and Nicolas Poussin and partly on 'Capability' Brown's native Northumberland scenery, replacing the formal patterns of earlier periods, but every element in it is in fact finely orchestrated. The house and the lake, the follies, temples and statues, the parkland and the river are all carefully arranged in relation to each other.

On Classic ground

Croome has an abundance of the picturesque elements that belong to the Georgian landscape garden style: the lake, broad sweeps of grass dotted with groves of trees, Neo-classical temples and statues. Many 18th-century

Above The Church is an 'eye-catcher', visible from many parts of the park

property owners had been on the Grand Tour to Italy, where they had seen the classical ruins and Tuscan landscapes that they would then attempt to reproduce in their gardens.

Exotics

In the case of the park, though, the groves of trees that dot the landscape were a cut above what might have been seen at other properties. Set out in 'Capability' Brown's trademark style as a series of different shrubberies that draw the eye, the trees here were often real rarities. The 6th Earl had a passion for collecting. He was one of the first to employ 'plant hunters', and when his friends went abroad, he asked them to bring back seeds. Some of the plants at Croome come from Captain James Cook's expeditions to the South Seas; others are from Russia and East Asia. 'Plant hunting' in the colonial era sometimes had a detrimental effect on the people and ecologies of the places where it occurred. The National Trust is working to understand how Croome's parkland connects to this history.

Detailed information about the 6th Earl's trees comes from an 1824 guidebook – *Hortus Croomensis* ('The Garden of Croome'), written by William Dean, the 7th Earl of Coventry's botanic gardener. Dean's grave was discovered several years ago. William Dean describes Croome as 'one of the largest and finest collections of Exotics in the kingdom,' and 'an exhibition of the vegetation of the Eastern and Western world, worthy the attention of the public'. He lists over 5,000 different plants growing in the park. By 1801, the collection was described by Arthur Young in the *Annals of Agriculture*, as 'second only to Kew' in its botanical diversity.

The National Trust has been methodically restoring the landscape, much of which had been turned over to intensive arable farming, since it acquired over 270 hectares (670 acres) of the park in 1996. While doing so, Dean's guide has been an invaluable reference.

Firsts of their kind

Among the unusual trees in the park are ginkgos, examples of which were extremely rare in 18th-century Britain. There is also a particularly large cedar of Lebanon, which is thought to be one of the oldest of its kind in the country and is likely to be one of the few trees at Croome that predates 'Capability' Brown's plantings.

View lines and the Wilderness Walk

Approaching the house from the Visitor Centre, you first get a glimpse of how it is set within the landscape.

Focal points

Croome's landscape gives an impression of nature, seemingly unconstrained. There are sweeping views instead of the rigid lines of formal gardens – older buildings that got in the way of the all-important view lines were simply demolished. There is a man-made lake and river, statues and temples, with the house as their central focus. The other buildings around the park include gatehouses, a grotto, a church and buildings termed 'eye-catchers', which are set far away from the house, and are intended to draw the eye into the wider landscape. In various places a ha-ha – that is, a concealed ditch, said to be named after the sound of surprise that visitors make when they stumble upon it – helps keep grazing animals out of the shrubberies without interrupting the view.

'And here, gradually opening before the surprised and delighted viewer – stretching in a wide circumference – appears a scene of rural beauty and grandeur, rarely surpassed; in which wood, water and ornamental buildings, aided by some pleasing inequalities of ground, combine to produce a finely picturesque and powerful effect.'

Hortus Croomensis, 1824

'The Stranger is next conducted into the Wilderness Walk – winding among the natural columns of closely-planted trees; twisting their branches together, in many a rude and fantastic form; and extending a rich canopy of foliage, over the head. It is a pleasant retreat – at all times, agreeable – but, in the glare of noon-day, in the heat of summer, it must be peculiarly refreshing and delightful.'

Hortus Croomensis, 1824

Wilderness Walk

The Wilderness Walk is now the main entrance into the park. It was originally a meandering path on the edge of the pleasure grounds, densely planted with shrubs and trees leading down to the arboretum and flower garden, which are yet to be restored and opened. The wide paths were meant for carriage rides, a typical way to visit parkland in the 18th century. Croome's park was largely designed to be seen from a carriage, with follies seeming to emerge from shrubberies, only to disappear again. A network of winding paths achieves the same effect, leading from one viewing point to the next. It's done so skilfully that we just see the illusion, not the artifice involved in creating it.

Church Shrubbery and Church

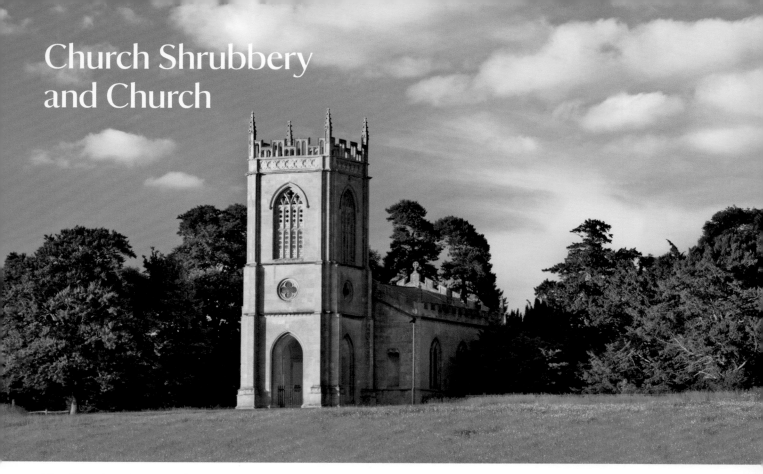

The Church at Croome shows the lengths that the 6th Earl was prepared to go to, to achieve his desired effect.

The 6th Earl and 'Capability' Brown considered the medieval church at Croome too close to the house, so it was demolished. The new Church, which incorporates interior masonry and timbers from the old one, was consecrated in 1763, on higher ground to make it an 'eye-catcher', visible from many parts of the park. It was designed by Brown in a 'pleasing and spirited imitation of the Gothic style'. The interior, meanwhile, was designed by Robert Adam in a delicate Georgian Gothic, with light plaster on the walls, though it has clear glass in the windows, rather than the stained glass that Adam had suggested.

The Church is consecrated to St Mary Magdalene, perhaps as a tribute to the 6th Earl's first wife, Maria Gunning, who is buried here. Apart from the arrangement of the pews, very little has changed inside since the 6th Earl's time. The parish is now too small to maintain such a building, so it is owned and looked after by the Churches Conservation Trust.

Tales from the crypt
The 6th Earl had the tombs of four of his 17th-century ancestors moved here from the demolished church and installed in the chancel. The bodies of the Coventrys, including the 6th Earl, are buried in a vault beneath the Church,

Above The 'Capability' Brown 18th-century church and Church Shrubbery which could be accessed via a secret passage at the side of the building, marked with the words *Candide et Constanter*, the family motto. Not all of the bodies of his ancestors appear to have been moved, however, so it is assumed that there are many more still under the soil near the house.

Church Shrubbery and Ice House

Within the Church Shrubbery is the domed brick Ice House, which was used to store winter ice for use in the house. The thatched roof was partly a decorative touch to make the building blend in with its surroundings but it also fulfilled a practical function of keeping it cool. More than two thirds of the building is below ground. The depth of the Ice House is 24 feet, which is a surprising drop. The Ice House worked rather like a thermos flask. The walls are double-skinned, and ice would have been taken from a nearby pond in winter and packed into the chamber, which was lined with straw for extra insulation. Throughout the summer the ice from the Ice House would have been used to preserve food and cool drinks as well as to create ice creams and sorbets.

The Ice House was in use up until 1915, and has now been restored after being found hidden in undergrowth, filled to the top with rubble.

'Leaving the Church – the Stranger will naturally pause – to contemplate, from its high grounds, the grand prospect, which again bursts, in full display, before him – offering a good near view of the House, seated in the vale below – thence extending over the lawns, the woods, and the waters, of the park – shut in by the long waving line of the Malvern hills, melting into the wide horizon.'

Hortus Croomensis, 1824

Above **Robert Adam's delicate interior**

Left **The restored Ice House**

The Home Shrubbery, Walled Garden and Stable Yard

Home Shrubbery

The Home Shrubbery is closest to the house, and is said to have been the 6th Earl's favourite place to walk. Planted with beautiful specimen trees, including ginkgos, cedars, and what at the time was considered Britain's finest *Magnolia grandiflora*, it was a place to be shown off to visitors. There was an aviary here too, and coffee, cinnamon and many other tropical plants were grown in a hothouse, of which only the foundations now remain. The two urns here are dedicated to the 6th Earl after his death and to George III, who visited Croome in 1788.

Walled Garden

At almost three hectares (seven acres), Croome's walled garden is the largest 18th-century walled garden in Britain. Like many parts of Croome it was left to overgrow in the 20th century, and by the time it was purchased by its current owners, Chris and Karen Cronin, it was in ruin. Since 2000 the Walled Garden has been subject to a major repair and restoration project by the Cronin family and it is now open regularly to visitors to Croome, in partnership with the National Trust.

The Coventry family evidently had a long interest in plants and gardens as the Walled Garden appears to originate in the early 18th century, when the 4th Earl made massive changes to the house and garden. The earliest plan of the Walled Garden dates from about 1750. Shortly after this, the 6th Earl and 'Capability' Brown made further changes. Hothouses were built for melons, pineapples, peaches and vines, a circular stone-curbed dipping pond was created and Robert Adam designed a sundial.

What makes the Walled Garden at Croome unique is not just its size, but the fact that the original records still survive, almost in their entirety, showing which plants were bought for it and how much they cost. This makes it of great importance to garden history. A bill from 1752 shows '100 artichokes, 1 doz. red currants, 4 doz. white, 5 doz. gooseberries and 20 vines' were purchased for the garden.

Left The magnificent walk through the Home Shrubbery

In 1806 a 13ft-high, free-standing 'hot wall' was built, heated by five furnaces day and night, to enable delicate fruit and flowers to be grown all year round. The 9th Earl had a fresh carnation for his buttonhole every day, even in winter.

Stable Yard

Adjoining the Walled Garden is the large and finely built brick Stable Yard, walled in on three sides. The size and importance of this building shows how horses were an essential part of life on the Croome estate before mechanisation. The stable buildings were converted into private homes, prior to the National Trust's involvement with Croome Court.

Left A door with hanging wisteria in the Walled Garden

Above The rose garden in the Walled Garden

The Rotunda

The domed Rotunda is a beautiful summer pavilion, and one of the earliest and most ornate garden buildings at Croome.

Positioned close to Croome Court, the building was designed by 'Capability' Brown as a 'garden room'. It was used to take tea and originally there was a circular dining table in the middle.

The Rotunda lies at the end of the Home Shrubbery, and is shrouded in trees, planted at Brown's suggestion.

Room with a view

The Rotunda is made more special by its position, high up on a ridge, giving it beautiful panoramic views of the parkland to the south, and the Malvern Hills to the west. From here it is also possible to see the 'eye-catchers' of Dunstall Castle and the Park Seat.

When the National Trust took on the care of the building, it was found that all the wooden beams inside the Rotunda's roof had rotted away. After being left in a state of neglect for decades, the Rotunda has now been restored to something of its former glory.

'Seated on its proud eminence, the ROTUNDA presents itself to view... It is an elegant stone building; plain in its exterior, but richly ornamented within: furnished with sofas, and fitted-up, as a summer evening apartment. A pleasing assemblage of trees, among which are the cypress and the cedar of Lebanon, form with their blended foliage a woody crescent, encircling and sheltering it. But its great charm is its fine prospect.'

Hortus Croomensis, 1824

Above The Rotunda sits high on a ridge overlooking the park

Left A detail of the restored interior

Right The trees which surround the Rotunda include Brown's signature, the cedar of Lebanon

The River and Lake

It may not be glamorous, but the fact that there is a park at Croome at all, instead of a marsh, is due to 'Capability' Brown's understanding of drainage, and his talent for water management.

Croome's central plain was originally a boggy, low-lying area, with a stream meandering through it. Beneath the surface of the parkland are miles of drainage tunnels, called culverts, built with around one and a half million bricks. Some of these culverts are visible today. Together with the new river and lake that Brown created, the culverts transformed what was originally a 'deep, dead, fetid morass' and 'a tract of naked barrenness' into parkland and farmland.

'A tract of naked barrenness'

The River

The river is the key to the Croome landscape. Before 'Capability' Brown arrived here, a short section of canal had been dug near to the house. Brown extended it, and made it flow in a serpentine arc, the 'line of beauty' that was so admired in the 18th century. Supposedly it is a scaled-down version of the River Severn, which flows a mile to the west, and even gives the illusion of running to join it. It took years to dig

Left A culvert, the key to 'Capability' Brown's water management

and large parts of its lower structure were discovered when the river was recently dredged. The original bridge only lasted for about a century. It was gone by the 1840s.

The Lake

At the west end of the river is the lake, in what had been a particularly boggy spot known as Seggy Mere. The lake is the 'grand receptacle' of some of the hidden culverts and drains that stop the park from turning back into a marsh. The lake is also the focus of what were known as the 'pleasure grounds', which in the 6th Earl's time were the setting for al fresco banquets and firework displays. Here a series of paths lead from one viewing point to another, where the trees, Grotto and Island Pavilion can be seen reflected in the lake.

The lake was dug out entirely by hand, and Brown probably spread the soil that was removed in the process over the fields at Croome, making unproductive land fertile. Originally, visitors crossed over the lake by means of a ferry, pulled by a rope. It is still possible to see the steps of the landing point close to the Dry Arch Bridge.

A question of taste

The Chinese Bridge that crossed the river was one of the few features in the park that were here before 'Capability' Brown, though the one you can see now is a reconstruction. By the 19th century many people thought that it was out of place in a naturalistic setting. According to the *Hortus Croomensis* in 1824, 'this sort of Bridge, of which Brown was too fond, modern taste would reject as too light in form, and too glaring in appearance, to suit with the grandeur of our English park scenery'.

the river out by hand, and Brown was careful to give it gently sloping banks, so that the 6th Earl's pedigree cattle could come down and drink from it in a picturesque manner.

It's known what the original Chinese Bridge looked like from two artworks, a design by the architect William Halfpenny, and a Richard Wilson painting made in 1758, which can be seen in the Drawing Room in Croome Court. The bridge's original abutments have been found,

Around the Lake

The many lakeside follies at Croome bear witness to the extravagance of the 6th Earl, and the Arcadian fantasy that he was trying to create.

Lakeside Urn and Boathouse

Designed by Robert Adam, the large limestone urn by the lake is decorated with rams' heads and garlands of flowers, giving it a pastoral feel.

Only brick foundations remain of the thatched boathouse that also lies at the head of the lake. Boating was a favourite pastime of the 6th Earl, who used to take his guests out in a pleasure barge, painted in the blue and vermilion livery of the Coventry family.

Island Pavilion

The Island Pavilion, which stands on one of the islands in the lake, can be reached via two 18th-century iron bridges. The Pavilion has been carefully restored, having been badly vandalised during years of neglect. The central plaque inside shows a Grecian wedding scene and is made of Coade stone.

Above The Island Pavilion

Left The elaborate Lakeside Urn

Grotto

No 18th-century landscape garden was complete without its grotto. The one at Croome is likely to have been designed by 'Capability' Brown, and is made out of volcanic tufa and limestone. Unlike some others, though, it seems that it was never home to a real-life hermit, perhaps because it was too small. Originally its walls would have been decorated with crystals of quartz, Blue John and other semi-precious stones, as well as fossils, pieces of coral and shells. Most of these have long since been stolen, despite gates being installed over the entrance in the 19th century.

The statue here is of Sabrina, whom the medieval chronicler Geoffrey of Monmouth described as a water nymph inhabiting the River Severn. Grottoes were traditionally the home of water nymphs which is why there is an inscription, taken from Virgil's *Aeneid*, which translates as 'Behold! A cave beneath the overhanging rocks. Inside, fresh-water springs, and seats formed from the living stone. This is the home of the Nymphs.' At night the statue of Sabrina would have been lit by a lamp hanging from an iron hook, which can still be seen today.

'Beyond the Grotto, appears the figure of a Water Nymph, reclining on the bank, and holding an urn – through which the waters, collected from a copious spring, at some distance, are made to flow.'
Hortus Croomensis, 1824

Below A classic example of an 18th-century grotto

The Dry Arch Bridge and the Druid

Several of Croome's garden features are made from Coade stone, which made the fortune of one of the 18th-century's foremost businesswomen.

Dry Arch Bridge

The Dry Arch Bridge allowed people to walk to the lake without having to dodge the many carriages on the busy drive which led to Croome from Worcester. The Coade stone keystones on the bridge feature the heads of river gods.

Druid

As well as classical motifs, many 18th-century landscape gardens contained reminders of Britain's ancient past. In Croome's case there is a statue of a Druid, with a pedestal designed by James Wyatt after Brown's death. Druids were seen as symbolising an ancient tradition of native British liberty, holding out against the Romans and subsequent invaders.

Set in stone

Both the Druid and the Dry Arch Bridge are made of Coade stone, a type of stoneware that can be cast into statues and other garden ornaments. It looks like Portland stone and, like Portland stone, is weather-resistant, staying clean no matter what the British climate throws at it.

'The figure of a DRUID soon appears; resting on a pedestal; and placed under the shade of a large oak; a tree, which, it is well known, the priests of that ancient order held in high veneration.'

Hortus Croomensis, 1824

Below The Coade stone statue of a Druid

Left The footpath to the lake leads underneath the Dry Arch Bridge

An old artificial stone recipe was perfected by Eleanor Coade, one of the 18th century's very few female entrepreneurs. Her company produced a vast range of ornaments in her factory in Lambeth, where the Royal Festival Hall now stands. Eleanor Coade's success as a businesswoman was very rare in the Georgian era. In fact she was one of the few people to succeed in the artificial stone business, thanks to a combination of managerial skills, hard work, entrepreneurial flair, and a talent for marketing and public relations.

Croome's collection of Coade stone statuary, placed throughout the grounds, is one of the largest and most important in the country. Following its introduction to Croome by 'Capability' Brown, when the 'Tablets of a Grecian Wedding' were inserted in the Island Pavilion, the 6th Earl seems to have developed a taste for the new material.

Worcester Gates

The Worcester Gates, flanking the old road from Worcester, were originally four stone pillars added by Brown. After Brown's death, James Wyatt adapted the pillars to create two archways and added the Coade stone urns on top, which give the gates their alternative name, the Punch Bowl Gates.

The 'Destroyer'
The third of the big names in design that are associated with Croome, James Wyatt was best known as an architect for his work on such Gothic Revival constructions as Fonthill Abbey in Wiltshire. His rather heavy-handed renovations of older buildings at some other sites earned him the nickname 'the Destroyer', but at Croome he added a great deal, such as the two-storey 'eye-catcher', the Panorama Tower.

Above One of the Punch Bowl Gates on the Worcester Road

Left Coade inscription on Sabrina's urn

The Evergreen Shrubbery and Temple Greenhouse

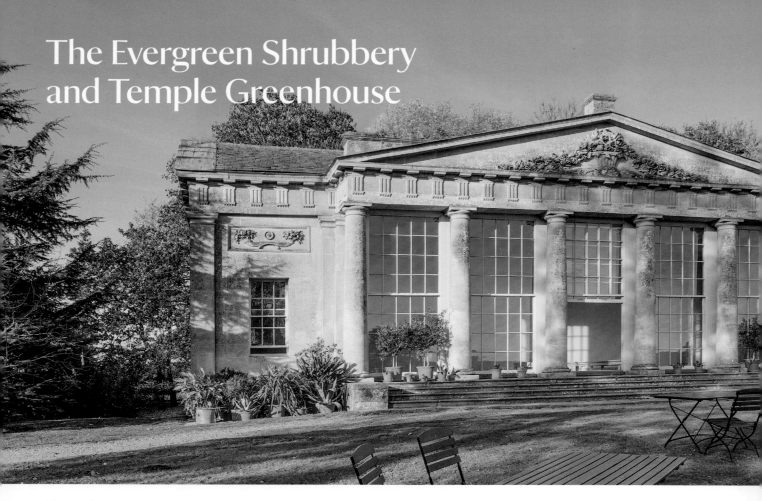

The path from the Temple Greenhouse back to the church passes the spot where a village once stood.

Temple Greenhouse

The Temple Greenhouse was Robert Adam's first garden building at Croome. He charged £15 for the design, which included designs for garden furniture, such as benches with lion's-paw feet, to go inside. The large windows, replacements of the lost originals, are designed to be removable so that they can be taken out in the summer months. The building housed some of the 6th Earl's collection of exotic plants. The carvings, by Sefferin Alken, of overflowing fruit and flowers, and horns of plenty, on the pediment outside, gave a taste of the abundance within. It was heated in the winter by a fire that was lit in a brick bothy at the back, with the heat then being channelled through voids in the floor. In niches where the smaller windows are now, there were originally lead sculptures of Flora and Ceres, goddesses of flowers and the harvest.

Near the Temple Greenhouse are the foundations of an 18th-century privy, for garden visitors who were caught short, now the location of a composting toilet for 21st-century visitors.

Above The Temple Greenhouse was a folly with a practical function

Right The restored statue of Pan

Far right Inside the Temple Greenhouse

'Delightfully sheltered, beneath the umbrageous arms of spreading trees, appears an elegant modern TEMPLE, open in front, supported by plain Doric pillars; from each side of which, the pleasure grounds are seen, extending in a long range.'

Hortus Croomensis, 1824

Pan

On the way from the Temple Greenhouse is the statue of Pan, restored after its headless body was found in the undergrowth several years after the National Trust took over the park. In the days before the lawnmower, sheep would have played an important part in keeping the grass short in the park so it's fitting to have a statue of the classical god of sheep and shepherds placed here.

Evergreen Shrubbery

The curving path from the Temple Greenhouse was planted with evergreens to keep it dark and mysterious. The shrubbery has been replanted, but not exactly as Brown intended. One area is

'That great patron of rural pursuits and rural pleasures [Pan] would have no cause to be dissatisfied with the situation in which a figure of himself is placed.'

Hortus Croomensis, 1824

prone to flooding, and the National Trust discovered that the planting here was partly removed in the late 18th century to allow for this. Statues of the Four Seasons used to stand here to provide interest, but they were stolen in the 1980s.

Relocation, relocation, relocation

Originally there were a few dwellings at the foot of the hill. They were demolished because they interrupted the sightlines in the park. The occupants were rehoused in a new settlement nearby, called Croome Village. In the 19th century the village was renamed High Green and many of the houses were extended. Bits of brick and tile still occasionally come to light at the spot where the original houses stood.

The Outer Eye-catchers

If you have the time, Croome's more far-flung follies are well worth a visit.

The Park Seat
Designed by Robert Adam, the Park Seat was built as a shelter and a viewing point. It is also known as the Owl's Nest, after a former occupant.

The Worcester Lodge
This gatehouse, which was designed by James Wyatt, sat on the main road to Croome from Worcester. The carriage drive ran from here, through the Worcester (or Punch Bowl) Gates located behind the Grotto, and on to the house beyond. Both sides of the carriage drive were densely planted with trees and shrubs, to delay the moment, for dramatic effect, when visitors first caught sight of the house. The driveway no longer exists, though, and the Lodge, which is privately owned, is now cut off from the rest of the park by the M5 motorway.

Pirton Castle
Dramatic Pirton Castle is situated on Pirton Ridge, to the north of Croome, and is flanked by cedars of Lebanon. This is a true folly. While it looks as though it was originally a castle, it was constructed as a ruin. With its crumbling Gothic walls, it is the perfect embodiment of the 18th-century trend of melancholy decay and picturesque decrepitude. Ironically, before the National Trust took Croome on, this building had been in a state of very real deterioration for many decades.

'The ruins of Pirton Castle… occupy a fine situation, on a lofty eminence; commanding from its high grounds, beautiful and extensive prospects.'
Hortus Croomensis, 1824

Left **The Park Seat**
Right **Dunstall Castle**
Far right **Panorama Tower**

Panorama Tower

The Panorama Tower, which was also designed by James Wyatt, is situated on Knight's Hill on the outskirts of the original park. This two-storey building has a fine staircase inside leading up to a circular viewing balcony, which looks out to the Malvern Hills. The Panorama Tower is now separated from Croome's park by the motorway.

Dunstall Castle

Standing on Dunstall Common, a mile south of the house, this is another mock-medieval folly. As its designer, Robert Adam, wrote to the 6th Earl, 'I think it might be built to have a good effect at a Distance at no great Expense, as there does not require much delicacy in the workmanship.' Though shrouded by trees, its tower can be seen from the Rotunda, after a major restoration by the National Trust restored the castle to its original height.

'The ingenious designer, Mr Brown'

Lancelot 'Capability' Brown's work at Croome made his reputation, and he was never to surpass it.

Lancelot Brown was nicknamed 'Capability', because he would typically tell his clients that their estates had great capabilities for improvement. He had worked at Stowe in Buckinghamshire for ten years as Head Gardener, helping to develop a new, more natural style of landscape under the influence of the designer William Kent. The 6th Earl of Coventry, having had Brown recommended to him by his friend, the gentleman architect Sanderson Miller, was the first to take him on after Brown chose to set up his own business. At Croome, Brown was able to take the ideas formed at Stowe and perfect them.

My Place and my Pocket

Brown started work at Croome in 1751, but he was employed first as an architect and not a landscape designer. Croome Court is a rare example of Brown's work on a house. He called it his 'first flight into the realms of architecture'. As well as being architect for the exterior of the building, he was clerk of works for the interior. Brown would return to Croome again and again over 30 years, calling it 'my first and most favoured child'.

Genius of place

For his part, Brown compared his role as a landscape designer to that of a poet, using his art to bring out the 'genius of place' in each location he transformed. 'Here I put a comma – there,

Above The Temple Greenhouse sits within Brown's sweeping landscape

Left Lancelot 'Capability' Brown by Nathaniel Dance, c.1773

from dining at the Earl's London house when he died on the doorstep of his daughter Bridget's house, on 6 February 1783.

Clearly, the 6th Earl had seen something in the budding designer, whose ideas so closely matched his own. His decision may have been helped by the fact that using Brown, new on the scene and relatively untried, would have been a comparatively cheap option. Soon after employing him, the 6th Earl was to write in typically parsimonious terms: 'Mr Brown has done very well by me, and indeed I think has studied both my Place and my Pocket, which are not always conjunctively the Objects of Prospectors.'

Inimitable and creative genius
Brown's memorial can be seen by the lake. It was damaged by a falling tree in 1972, but has since been restored. It reads, 'To the memory of Launcelot Brown, who, by the powers of his inimitable and creative genius, formed this garden scene out of a morass.'

when it's necessary to cut the view, I put a parenthesis; there I end it with a period and start on another theme.'

At Croome, Brown was able to develop what was to become his signature style. His smooth expanses of undulating grass running straight to the house, clumps of trees, and serpentine lakes formed by invisibly damming small rivers, were something new within England – a 'gardenless' form of landscape gardening that swept away the formal patterns of previous ages. Brown would go on to create at least 170 others in a similar vein.

From their working relationship, a genuine friendship developed between 'Capability' Brown and the 6th Earl. Indeed the Earl was probably the last person to speak to Brown, who was returning

'Bob the Roman'

The renowned Neo-classical architect, interior and furniture designer Robert Adam created his first complete room design at Croome Court.

Robert Adam probably met the 6th Earl in 1759 and started to create designs for Croome in 1760. This was two years after he returned from Italy, where he had studied the surviving monuments of antiquity. He had also been strongly influenced by the imaginative visions of the artist Giovanni Battista Piranesi, whom he befriended. Soon he had set up in business with his brother James, advertising his services as a designer of complete schemes for the decoration and furnishing of houses. The new, classical architectural style that he developed would come to dominate British taste for the next two decades.

From churches to commodes

Adam's first commission at Croome wasn't for a classical design but, ironically, for a Gothic one: the interior of the new church at Croome. Adam's delicate Georgian Gothic design was applied to the plasterwork on the ceiling, as well as to the pulpit, font, doors, floor and pews. He even provided a design for the stained glass, which was never executed.

So pleased was the 6th Earl with Adam's work that more commissions came his way, including several of Croome Court's interiors, this time in a Neo-classical style. The Long Gallery at Croome is thought to be Adam's first complete room design, covering everything from the ceiling, plasterwork, mirrors and chimneypiece to the furniture and decorative grisailles. He even designed commodes in the classical style.

Adam also designed many of the temples and follies in the park, including the Temple Greenhouse, Dunstall Castle, the Park Seat and the London Arch and many unexecuted designs. 'Bob the Roman', as he was jokingly called, having immersed himself in the Eternal City, would work at Croome for over 30 years, as well as transforming the 6th Earl's London town house in Piccadilly.

We know that there was some give and take between the two men, with the 6th Earl rejecting some of Adam's designs or the occasional argument about bills, but both client and architect remained on good terms. When Adam died, the 6th Earl was one of his pallbearers at Westminster Abbey.

Left A detail of
a chimneypiece in the
Saloon

Far left Robert Adam
attributed to George
Willison, c.1770–1775

Above A detail of a
chimneypiece in the
Long Gallery

Fertile genius
In his obituary, *The Gentleman's Magazine* praised Robert Adam's 'fertile genius in elegant ornament' and said that he had 'produced a total change in the architecture of this country'.

Croome Court

Following the Second World War, the mansion house at Croome had a chequered history.

Croome Court, the principal building at Croome, had been the home of the Coventry family since the 16th century, though the building in its current form was started in 1751.

The 6th Earl set about transforming the red brick, 17th-century house of his ancestors, but he didn't knock it down, perhaps for reasons of economy or sentiment. Instead he used it as a template, altering and refacing it in the Palladian style, but using the old foundations, and keeping some of the walls that form the central spine of the house. That is why, unlike many other Palladian mansions, Croome Court does not occupy a commanding position up on high ground, such as where the Church now stands.

Brown added new turreted wings at each end, and a magnificent Palladian portico was built on the southern side. Traces of the original building can still be seen inside, however, and the chimneystacks from the older building are visible above the roof.

Interesting times

In 1948, the Croome Estate Trust had to sell Croome Court, along with almost all of its original furniture and fittings. The 10th Earl had been killed on the retreat to Dunkirk in 1940, and with maintenance costs rising and agriculture depressed, the upkeep of Croome Court could no longer be supported by the great estate surrounding it.

The sale was arranged through the Croome Estate Trust, which had been set up by George William, the 9th Earl (1838–1930), to try to protect Croome's legacy. We also have the 9th Earl to thank for the fact that the fabric of the Court has remained relatively unchanged since the 18th century. As Earl for some 87 years, he ensured that the house escaped many Victorian additions and he is said to have prided himself on the fact that the house had not been decorated since the 1780s.

Above The south-facing facade of Croome Court

A new start

In October 2007, Croome Court, now suffering after years of neglect, was bought by the Croome Heritage Trust, which was created as an offshoot of the Estate Trust. They took the property on in partnership with the National Trust, which undertook to run and repair it. The house opened to the public on 26 September 2009 and the Heritage Trust have since extended the lease to the National Trust for 999 years.

Blank canvas

With about four-fifths of its collection absent, Croome Court isn't presented as a traditional National Trust property. Instead, rooms are used to present temporary exhibitions and installations created by up-and-coming artists, craftspeople and designers, continuing the 6th Earl's legacy of nurturing new talent.

After the Second World War, Croome Court was used as a school (1950s–1979) and later (1979–84) as the UK headquarters for the International Society for Krishna Consciousness. It was then not lived in for 12 years, as it was bought and sold by a succession of property developers, who tried, unsuccessfully, to turn Croome into a country club, hotel and a golf course. In 1998 another property developer turned the house into a private home once more, living here with his family.

The Main Hall and Billiard Room

The entrance to Croome Court is carefully designed to create a dramatic effect.

As you approach the house, you begin to see its creamy Bath stone and roof of Westmorland slate. Croome Court is built in the Palladian style, named after the Venetian architect Andrea Palladio, whose work aspired to the symmetry of classical temple architecture.

Near miss
Entering the house, you pass under a stone carving of the family crest of the Earls of Coventry. This nearly altered the course of British parliamentary history, when a stone jewel from the crown of the crest fell down in the 1920s, narrowly missing the future Prime Minister Stanley Baldwin who was visiting his friend, the 9th Earl.

Main Hall
Before the house was remodelled in the 18th century, the Main Hall was much larger than the room that you see now. The smaller size reflects the reduced status of the room. It was used primarily as a waiting room, furnished with a row of chairs bearing the family crest, where visitors would wait to be admitted into the Saloon beyond. As a comparatively small space, it serves to fuel anticipation, and emphasises the drama of entering the much bigger Saloon, with its double-height ceiling, big south-facing windows, and rich decoration.

Billiard Room
The room to the right of the Main Hall as you enter the house was used as a Billiard Room in the 1750s, reflecting the 6th Earl's taste for what was a fashionable pastime. Croome appears to have had a billiard table from the beginning of the game's history, with one mentioned in a 1719 inventory. Another inventory, from shortly afterwards, mentions 'a Billiard Table' as well as '3 Pair of Balls, 5 Mahogany Cues and 14 other Cues'.

During Croome's time as a school, this was used as a classroom for the youngest children.

Right **Main Hall**

Croome's collection

Despite the losses incurred following the sale of the house and contents in 1948, enough of the original collection at Croome survives to highlight the sophisticated taste of the 6th Earl of Coventry. More than 40 different craftsmen were commissioned to create the interiors of the house, including furnishings and textiles by many of London's leading designers and cabinetmakers.

The 6th Earl's collection, including furniture, tapestries, paintings and books, was hugely significant and influential, even within his own lifetime. A passionate Francophile, the 6th Earl also shopped regularly in Paris and his avant-garde taste led the way which others could only emulate. Even Louis XV, King of France demanded a copy of the exquisite porcelain ewer and basin which the 6th Earl commissioned from the Sèvres porcelain factory in 1760 and which remains in the collection.

A pair of commodes, originally used as bedroom cupboards, are among the key pieces still remaining in the collection, now on loan from the Croome Estate Trust. Elaborately inlaid in satinwood, rosewood and holly, they were made in 1764 by furniture makers Mayhew & Ince at a cost of £40. The simple form, combined with elegant and innovative decoration in Neo-classical style, illustrates the range and quality of the collection.

The Long Gallery, Saloon and Drawing Room

The Long Gallery was Robert Adam's first complete room.

Long Gallery

Installed between 1761 and 1766, the Long Gallery takes up the western side of the ground floor. It is designed for looking outwards, with superb views over the Croome river to the Malvern Hills. Robert Adam designed everything in the original room, from the chimneypiece and mirrors to the furniture. Adam had originally thought that this room should be the library and he sent plans to the 6th Earl, but they were rejected. The drawings survive in the archive.

The ceiling in this room was Robert Adam's first. He used a design from a temple in Palmyra, Syria, but archive material in the Sir John Soane Museum in London shows that he couldn't get the pattern to match the space available at Croome. In particular, he was unable to extend the pattern seamlessly into the bay, and the design shows that he re-worked the area several times.

The Saloon

The Saloon is where George III had dinner when he visited Croome in 1788. Lampreys (eel-like fish) were among the items on the menu, and the 6th Earl is said to have committed a faux pas by keeping his hunting boots on during the meal. Still, the King seems to have had a good time. He later remarked to an acquaintance 'you can't conceive, sir, how we laughed and joked with Lord Coventry.'

When the 6th Earl died, he lay in state in the centre of this room, which was hung with black velvet. The Saloon is late Rococo in style, with lots of swirling leaf motifs, designed to bring the parkland motifs into the house. The chimneypieces in the Saloon were designed in the Neo-classical style.

'How we laughed and joked with Lord Coventry.'

King George III

Drawing Room

We know little about this room other than what appears in inventories. For example, paintings by Gainsborough, Zuccarrelli and Claude Gellée 'le Lorrain' once hung here, on walls covered first in blue and later yellow damask. The Richard Wilson landscape that hangs here now was painted in 1758 on the west bank of the river, looking back to the house. It is the very first illustration of a 'Capability' Brown landscape. When Wilson painted it, however, the park wasn't complete, and the church depicted hadn't yet been built.

Above *Croome Court, Worcestershire* by Richard Wilson c.1758

Left The Long Gallery, designed for looking out at the park

Far left The Long Gallery c.1915

Tapestry Room, Library and Lord Coventry's Dressing Room

These rooms vividly illustrate the way that Croome's fortunes have fluctuated.

Tapestry Room

This room was originally hung with some of the finest tapestries in Europe. In vibrant pink and gold, they were made by the Royal Gobelins manufactory in Paris. The adventurous 6th Earl was the first person outside of the French royal family to purchase tapestries in this series. They were the height of fashion, and he was prepared to seek the finest in the world for Croome. They took several years to be made to measure and were the pride of Croome Court. Eventually though, the tapestries were reluctantly sold, to cover the gambling debts of the 9th Earl's son.

The Croome tapestries are now in the Metropolitan Museum of Art in New York. In 1948, the rest of the room was sold and was cut up, packed into crates and shipped across the Atlantic. The Robert Adam-designed ceiling was cut up into two-foot sections along with the skirting boards, and even the floor. The room and tapestries are now reunited in the Met. At Croome today there is a 1949 replica of the original ceiling. On the walls, meanwhile, you can see the panelling that the tapestries were originally fixed on as well as some of the backing hessian and lining paper that once protected them.

Above The Tapestry Room, now in the Metropolitan Museum of Art in New York

Left Detail of a tapestry

Far right The bare panelling in the Tapestry Room at Croome today

Library

Grand bookcases, designed by Robert Adam, originally covered the entire wall space. This is where the 6th Earl kept his volumes on his favourite subjects: horticulture, architecture, botany and natural history. Many of these books were sold in 1948 and the bookcases were used for storing stationery when Croome was a boys' school. The Victoria and Albert Museum acquired these incredibly important bookcases in 1975 and are in the process of returning them to Croome on loan.

Lord Coventry's Dressing Room

This was a space for the 6th Earl to relax in, and get dressed for dinner in the Dining Room next door. It was positioned so that the Earl could see any visitors arriving via the drive and ensure that he was ready for his guests.

The wrong fit

The only piece of original furniture from the Tapestry Room that survives at Croome is a water stand designed by Robert Adam. The 6th Earl ordered the porcelain jug and basin from the Sèvres manufactory in Paris. The wooden stand, meanwhile, was made in London, but when stand and jug were finally finished and brought together, it was found that they didn't quite fit each other!

The Dining Room

The Dining Room shows some of the challenges facing the National Trust, in deciding how parts of Croome should be presented.

The plasterwork in this room, which includes stucco representations of the kinds of fruit and flowers that were grown in Croome's Walled Garden, was originally an off-white colour. When Hare Krishna devotees bought Croome in the late seventies, they painted the garlands in the bright colours you can see today. The walls in between were painted in aqua blue and salmon pink, but one of the Court's owners in the nineties said that the sight of them made his hangovers worse, so he painted the panels white! All of these varied colour schemes reflect periods of Croome's history. Which should the National Trust keep?

Croome and Krishna Consciousness

Prior to 1979, the headquarters of the International Society for Krishna Consciousness (ISKCON) in the UK were at Bhaktivedanta Manor near Watford in Hertfordshire, a large Victorian house given by George Harrison due to his interest in Indian culture and religion.

By the late 1970s, however, Bhaktivedanta Manor was becoming too small for the growing movement, and so ISKCON took the step of partially relocating to Worcestershire. They were to remain at Croome for five years.

During these years, Croome was renamed Chaitanya College, after a 16th-century Hindu saint and precursor of the Hare Krishna movement. There was a primary school for the children of devotees, and Croome became a worldwide centre for the training of students in Krishna consciousness. Chaitanya College was also a home base for devotees who travelled the country, a centre for the distribution of literature about ISKCON, and a quiet retreat. There were offices, meeting rooms, a shop and kitchen, a temple and living accommodation.

Left The brightly coloured garlands in the Dining Room

Far left Detail of the intricate decoration in the Dining Room

Above Sri Chaitanya Mahaprabhu, the namesake of Chaitanya College

Good omens

ISKCON member Sri Pati Das had looked at a number of stately homes as possible locations, but when he came to Croome, he watched a group of swans, seen as a bird of good omen, fly down and land on the river, and knew that Croome was the right house.

First Floor – East

The suite of rooms on the east side of the first floor includes a bedroom thought to have been used by the 6th Earl's first wife, Maria Gunning.

The general layout of the first floor mirrors that of the ground floor, with the rooms arranged along a long central corridor. When the house was remodelled for the 6th Earl, one of the rooms on this floor was lost, to make space for the double-height Saloon below. All of the public staterooms at Croome were on the ground floor, so the architectural decoration on the first floor tended to be simpler.

Chinese Bedroom

Once decorated in 'chinoiserie' style, fashionable in the 18th century, this was the principal bedroom of the 6th Earl's first wife, Maria, who is thought to have died in this room while the house was still being built. On the walls were 'a fine and rare set of eighteenth-century Chinese wallpaper hangings, painted in polychrome, with imaginative scenes set in a landscape of mountains, rivers and islands'. In 1949 this Chinese wallpaper was sold at Sotheby's for just £50. This room was later used as a boys' dormitory during Croome Court's time as a school.

Paper money
While much of what happened inside Croome Court during the Second World War remains a mystery, there is a bill in the archive for £200, the equivalent of over £6,000 today, which was presented to the Ministry of Works for damaging the wallpaper in this room in the 1940s.

Right On the walls of the Chinese Bedroom today is a modern version of chinoiserie wallpaper

Far right Chimneypiece bought by the 9th Earl for his bedroom

The Boudoir

The room next to the Chinese Bedroom, in the south-east corner of the first floor, was originally a dressing room used by Maria Gunning, the 6th Earl's first wife. It housed a spectacular overmantel mirror, made by William Linnell, which was sold at auction in 2012 for over £300,000. Maria's tragic story, of the once-famous beauty ravaged by tuberculosis, did much to generate interest in the mirror into which she must have gazed.

In the public eye

Maria was thought to be so beautiful that she used to attract large crowds of people in Hyde Park who came to see her pass by. George II once sent his personal guard to protect her from mobs! A Worcester shoemaker is also said to have charged a penny, just for glimpses of the shoes he was mending for her.

First Floor – West

This series of rooms had included the 6th Earl's main bedroom, but subsequent history has left its mark.

Alcove Room

This room, which matches another on the north side of the house, was possibly the 6th Earl's bedroom before he was married. The panelling predates Brown's remodelling of the house, so it may be original to the room or have been brought in from somewhere else.

Master Bedroom

This was where the 6th Earl slept while he lived at Croome Court. Its decor, however, comes from an altogether different period. It was chosen by one of the property developers who owned Croome in the 1990s, and the National Trust has decided to leave it as it was during this period for now. Variously described as an example of 1990s 'bling', or as something out of *Footballers' Wives* or *Hello!* magazine, the walls are covered in stripy black and tan wallpaper. In this room and in the adjoining space, the late 20th-century history of the house is explored.

Above **The 1990s Bathroom**

Left **The two tower rooms, now the accessible stores, used to be children's bedrooms in the 1990s and have now been redecorated**

Master bathroom

Today's adjoining bathroom was once the bedroom of the 6th Earl's second wife, Barbara St John, and a door leads to the 6th Earl's bedroom next door. This was the original location of the first state bed to be designed by Robert Adam, parts of which still survive in the Croome collection.

Water, water everywhere

Of all the 1990s additions to this room, perhaps the most unfortunate was a large, square bath that was installed in the middle of the floor. The weight of a full bath is thought to have been partially responsible for the floor sagging underneath; it required urgent repair work when the National Trust took on the house. The bath is still here but no longer plumbed in!

Second Floor – Behind the scenes

The low-ceilinged rooms under the eaves at Croome were home to the small army of servants who kept the place running.

The second floor at Croome is accessible by guided tour.

The architectural detailing in this part of the house is notably simpler than elsewhere. In most rooms the ceilings are quite low, as they are partially set within the roof space. These rooms would have been used as servants' accommodation. When Croome was a school, this floor was out of bounds to the boys, as it was where the nuns (see p.49) had their sleeping quarters.

The largest space on the second floor was known as the 'lumber garret'. Its round window looks out over the top of the south portico, towards the southern part of the Croome park.

Above Under the eaves on the second floor

Right The second floor corridor

The Tower Rooms

The rooms on this floor were added during the rebuilding of the house in the 18th century. The Tower Rooms, one on each corner, are quite different from the rest of the second floor. They have high ceilings and large windows, providing fine views across the park. In the 18th century these rooms were where bachelor visitors would stay, while in the 19th century the Tower Rooms were used as bedrooms for ladies' maids.

Period features

The second floor rooms have a distinctive 17th-century character, as many of the fittings from the old house were left in place, or moved here from other parts of Croome Court when they became unfashionable. Nearly every door on this floor dates from this period.

Basement

This is the best place to discover the secrets of the old house, and to see traces from the time when Croome was a school.

During the 18th century, much was made of the fact that the grounds at Croome were created from a marsh, as if it symbolised the triumph of Enlightened rationality, emerging from chaos. The house, too, seems an embodiment of order, with its clean lines and harmonious proportions. But look closely, and you'll discover that it's not quite as ordered as it seems.

In the Basement it's possible to see how the Palladian building was built around the shell of a much older one. This was done partly to save money, as the 6th Earl was primarily interested in the parkland. There is a patchwork of old flagstones on the floor, including fine slabs which may have been from another building that originally stood nearby. There are blocked-up doors with the hinges still in place, and odd niches with no obvious purpose. A central spine

Above Croome Court school pupils and staff, August 1962

Left The Basement

Top right A 17th-century window uncovered in the Basement

wall, part of the older building, still runs through the house at this level. Openings have had to be knocked through it at various points, to allow access, and some of the windows, which look so regular from the outside, are in reality 'blind' as parts of the old house are blocking them. Elsewhere, there are further signs that the later additions to the house don't quite match up with the old. The wooden staircase, for example, doesn't fit with the windows, its landings being out of kilter.

A school for boys

After the Second World War, Croome Court was sold by the Croome Estate Trust to the Roman Catholic Archdiocese of Birmingham. It was adapted to become a Catholic junior boarding school for disadvantaged boys. From the fifties to the seventies boys from all over the country were taught here by nuns.

Traces of this time are visible in the Basement. You can still see the marks of shower cubicles on the floor in the Butler's Pantry. The small wooden lockers in the dry cellar, made in the school woodwork shop, were assigned to the boys to keep their possessions, including their clothes.

Some boys were here because they were orphans, others because they had suffered neglect or because they had learning difficulties. While for some pupils the experience of going to school in a place like Croome was an enjoyable one, for others it was very difficult.

Red Wing

Attached to the rest of the house, the Red Wing was home to Croome's servants – and the 6th Earl in his last years.

Two buildings that previously stood on the site of Croome Court had burnt down following fires which started in basement kitchens. So when the Palladian mansion came to be built, the kitchens were housed in a separate wing. It was made of red brick, a less expensive material than the Bath stone of the main house, and constructed on the site of an older service building.

Sad end

After the 6th Earl's second wife died in 1804, the Earl lived on for another five years occupying just two rooms on the first floor of the Red Wing, living practically as a recluse. It was a sad end for someone who had cut such a dash in his younger days, and who had seen the fame of his creation, Croome Court and its surrounding park, spread far and wide.

Up from the ruins

When the National Trust acquired Croome, the Red Wing had been lying in ruin. The windows had been taken out by a previous owner, which meant that the rain got in, and it was possible to look up through three storeys to the sky through a huge hole in the roof. With the help of English Heritage, the National Trust completed a million-pound project to repair and rescue the building.

Left and top right
The interior of the Red
Wing before its rescue

A meeting of minds

Following the loss of his first wife, Lord Coventry remarried in 1764. Like his first wife, his new bride, Barbara St John, was also a great beauty, but she and the 6th Earl seemed to be completely in tune with each other. The new Countess of Coventry took an active part in tracking down rare plants for the garden, and she was also interested in birds and animals. She helped to create the menagerie at Croome, which was accessed through a wood that is now cut in two by the M5 motorway. The menagerie featured 'Sparrows of Paradise, Red-headed Parakeets, a Snow Bird and Silver Pheasants.' The 6th Earl and the Countess spent 40 happy years together.

Wartime Croome

The Second World War left its mark, both on Croome and on the Coventry family.

In May 1940, the 10th Earl of Coventry was killed in action during the retreat to Dunkirk. Later that year much of the eastern part of the park was requisitioned to form part of a new RAF station. Originally part of Bomber Command, it later became a top secret airbase developing airborne radar.

RAF Defford, as it was called, was built originally as a satellite of the nearby Pershore Airfield, where bomber crews were trained. It then became the base for the Telecommunications Flying Unit, established to test various types of radar equipment being developed at the nearby Telecommunications Research Establishment in Malvern. The Telecommunications Flying Unit had originally been based at Hurn on the south coast, but after the Battle of Britain it was moved here, to be out of range of enemy attack.

Visitor Centre

Some of the renovated RAF Defford buildings, including the Airmen's Ward, the Medical Inspection Block and the Decontamination Chamber, now serve as the National Trust's Visitor Centre and Canteen.

These buildings, which are the first structures seen by visitors to Croome, are the last remaining buildings of what was a much larger base. RAF Defford's runways, which are about a mile away, are still largely there, though they are no longer used. The surviving buildings made up the base's Sick Quarters, which were used to treat minor illnesses, to provide accident and emergency cover for the airfield, and to deal with potential casualties in the event of gas attack. These may be the only complete sick quarters of this type in the country.

A museum that tells the story of RAF Defford is housed in the base's former Decontamination Annexe and Ambulance Garage, and work is ongoing to save the other former RAF buildings on the site.

Above Enjoy a cuppa in the 1940s-style restaurant

Left Many of the original signs from the Second World War can still be seen around the Visitor Centre

Far left (above) The Visitor Centre

Far left (below) The Visitor Centre before its restoration. Two more buildings are still to be restored

Living memories

Much of what happened at Croome in the Second World War was shrouded in secrecy.

RAF Defford was such a closely guarded secret that even people living near here, or working at RAF Pershore nearby, didn't know the purpose of the base.

Airborne radar was tested and evaluated here during and after the war, enabling crews to identify enemy planes, detect ships and submarines at sea, or find their targets on bombing operations.

It was dangerous work. Between 1942 and 1955 there were 50 fatalities resulting from crashes involving aeroplanes based at RAF Defford. There is a memorial for these casualties on the village green in nearby Defford. In 1945 RAF Defford also saw a Boeing 247-D carry out the first fully automatic approach and landing, which paved the way for modern aircraft being able to land safely in any weather.

Around 2,700 servicemen and women were stationed here at the height of the base's activity, and reunions are still held for veterans. The airfield closed in 1957, as its runways were too short for the larger jet bombers that were coming into service.

Royal visitors?

Croome Court was occupied briefly by Queen Wilhelmina of the Netherlands during the war, though this is only hearsay, as the extreme secrecy of the time means that there are very few records. Croome was also identified as one of five possible refuges for the British royal family, in the event of an invasion.

Above Lancaster with 'A' Flight personnel

Left Ground crew with Wellington fitted with ASV radar

Right (above) Control tower at RAF Defford

Right (below) A group of officers c.1946

Safety in uniform
When scientists from the Telecommunications Research Establishment went on test flights behind enemy lines, they dressed as RAF officers because if they were shot down, they didn't want the enemy to think that they were spies.

Afterword

When the National Trust took over the parkland at Croome in 1996, the lake and river were filled with silt, statues were lost in undergrowth, and many buildings were almost in ruin. After the Second World War, much of Croome's parkland and several of Brown's shrubberies were ploughed to grow crops. The remaining shrubberies were overgrown. Over £8 million has been raised to help restore the park, and many volunteers have also donated their time and energy.

Forty-five thousand trees and shrubs have been replanted using information from old estate bills, and from William Dean's 1824 guidebook. Over 400 acres of intensively farmed arable land has been returned to wildflower meadow and pasture. Fifty thousand cubic metres of silt have been removed from the river and lake, and as perhaps 'Capability' Brown did when the lake was first dug out, the National Trust spread the silt over the fields, leaving just the clay-lined bowl of the river to stop the water draining away. Croome's outer 'eye-catchers' have also been acquired and restored.

Croome Court was leased to the National Trust in 2007, and the massive programme of repair began shortly afterwards. New plumbing, electrics and heating have been installed throughout the building, and the structure of the house has been repaired. The remaining parts of the internationally important Coventry collection of furniture and works of art have finally been brought home and the Red Wing, which stands cheek-by-jowl with Croome Court, has been saved from the threat of complete dereliction.

After decades of separation, the Palladian mansion and its designed landscape, the two halves of the same whole, have finally been brought back together again as 'Capability' Brown, Robert Adam and the 6th Earl originally intended.

Above Croome's park and house once again sit in harmony with each other